Beneath So Kind a Sky

CHURCH OF THE HOLY TRINITY, GRAHAMVILLE. *1860*

Beneath So Kind a Sky

The Scenic and Architectural Beauty

of South Carolina

Photographs by

CARL JULIEN

Introduction by

CHAPMAN J. MILLING

Thank Him who placed us here
Beneath so kind a sky
—HENRY TIMROD

UNIVERSITY OF SOUTH CAROLINA PRESS • COLUMBIA

First Printing, 1947

Second Printing, 1948

Third Printing, 1956

Fourth Printing, 1958

Fifth Printing, 1966

Sixth Printing, 1969

Standard Book Number: 87249–010–6
Library of Congress Catalog Card Number: 48–4
Manufactured in the United States of America

First printed by The R. L. Bryan Company
Columbia, South Carolina

Original engravings by The Carolina Engraving Company
Columbia, South Carolina

Sixth Printing by Kingsport Press, Inc.
Kingsport, Tennessee

For Jessie

NOTES ON PLATES

Beneath So Kind a Sky

INTRODUCTION

THE PURPOSE of this book is to help everyone, natives included, to understand better the elements which compose the peculiar character and charm of South Carolina, so well loved but often so poorly comprehended.

Charlestonians are reputed to hold that civilization ends at Goose Creek. Many Up Countrymen are inclined to the belief that all Charlestonians are steeped in iniquity, especially around election day. As for outsiders, their case is all but hopeless. Some of them conceive of the whole state as a romantic Arcadia, where goateed old gentlemen in white spats perpetually renew their julep glasses. Others envision a hookworm-infested swamp peopled by morose illiterates who enjoy as their sole pastime the occasional excitement of a well-organized lynching. Some think the only scenery consists of eroded gullies, the only flora the chinaberry tree and the jimson weed. Still others picture the whole state as a semi-tropical paradise somewhat resembling a South Sea island.

The truth is that South Carolina consists of two distinct geographical regions, the Up Country and the Low Country. The Up Country is composed of a Piedmont section and a narrow strip of actual mountains. The Low Country starts with the tide-water and ends in the sand hills, with a broad, relatively even plain between. Each of these sections has its distinctive natural features and each its own culture.

Few South Carolinians know or love their state so well as Carl Julien. Certainly none has ever interpreted her so perfectly in photographic art. His lens has captured brilliant glimpses both of the romance of the Low Country and of the pioneer integrity of the Piedmont. Although an Up Countryman by birth, he knows no narrow sectionalism. As with every true South Carolinian there are cypresses and Spanish moss in his soul as well as maples and rhododendron.

From among the thousands of photographs which Carl Julien has made of South Carolina, the ninety-two included in this volume have been selected as being representative of his art while at the same time giving a balanced picture of the state. A few of South Carolina's famed show-places have been included, but others equally lovely have been omitted to make room for pictures of more humble dwellings, churches and scenes which even more truly represent the soul of the state. Nor has mere antiquity been a criterion for selection, although all buildings included have stood the test of time, most

[1]

of them far antedating the War for Southern Independence. Charleston has not been given the proportionate representation to which it is entitled simply because its charm has been so skillfully portrayed so many times, and scenes from other towns and counties have been omitted because of the limitations of space. But every section is represented by pictures of the woods, the swamps, the rivers, the ocean and the hills, all of which have left their stamp on man who has, in turn, expressed his finest feelings in the buildings he has erected.

It is with the hope that the reader may gain a better understanding of the geographical, social and historical setting of Carl Julien's pictures that this introduction is offered.

I

THE TIDEWATER region has eternal appeal for romanticists. It is a land of majestic rivers, of noble avenues of live oaks, of eye-filling sweeps of yellow-green marshes, of abandoned rice fields, of ruined churches and plantation houses. Here the scenery is something out of fairyland, as breath-taking to a native of Greenville as to a man from Ohio. Gaunt, rustling palmettos forming a jungle backdrop for a perfect beach; lush sub-tropical flora; exotic shore-birds wheeling and dipping over the surf; giant turtles lumbering across the sand to lay their eggs. All these and more are part of the eternal but ever-changing picture. Behind the beach there is usually a strip of forest, which sometimes comes perilously close to the ocean's edge. Here, where wind and tide fight their perpetual battle with organic nature, are to be found the maimed old veterans of the conflict, the dwarfed pines and cedars, the little gnarled live oaks no taller than a black-jack, all their boughs facing landward. Here are low, dense thickets of myrtle and cassena struggling to consolidate each nascent dune. Beyond the forest there are usually fields, once covered with long-staple cotton, now planted, if at all, in melons, cucumbers or garden truck. Bordering the rivers are the salt marshes, wide expanses of golden-green, waving and rippling with each breath of wind. It is here that the descendants of English, Barbadian and Huguenot settlers harnessed the tide, sweetened the salt flats with fresh river water and grew the golden rice which brought wealth and leisure to their children.

Back along the rivers and tidal creeks lie the pine and cypress forests. These are the dominant trees, but live oak, hickory and magnolia are plentiful as are the tulip tree (known everywhere in South Carolina as poplar), the black gum and the tupelo.

Everywhere one sees streamers of Spanish moss, giving the trees a somber appearance of age and dignity. Truly there is something about Spanish moss that brings to the thoughtful man an ennobling sense of his own brevity and insignificance.

Carpeting the forest floor is a dwarf type of palmetto, a clump of green fans without a trunk, and lurking in their humid shade is that sinister foe of man and beast, the diamond-back rattlesnake. Deer abound in this region, and it is also one of the last stands of the wild turkey.

Other and lesser game is still relatively abundant, the fox squirrel, the "cat" squirrel, the raccoon, the opossum and the humble rabbit. Coveys of quail—partridges to every true Carolinian—burst from the ground like rockets and sail unerringly to the thickest tangle of briars.

The waters abound with seafood of every variety: oysters, clams, flounders, mullet, shrimp and crabs in the creeks and inlets; rock bass, black bass, red breast and bream a little higher up.

Here is the impression of William Hilton, who explored the Carolina coast in September, 1663:

"The Land generally, except where the Pines grow, is a good Soyl, covered with black Mold, in some places a foot, in some places half a foot, and other places lesse, with Clay underneath mixed with Sand . . . The Indians plant in the worst Land because they cannot cut down the Timber in the best, and yet have plenty of Corn, Pompions, Water-Mellons, Musk-Mellons: although the Land be over grown with Weeds through their lasinesse, yet they have two or three crops of Corn a year, as the Indians themselves inform us. The Country abounds with Grapes, large Figs and Peaches; the Woods with Deer, Conies, Turkeys, Quails, Curlues, Plovers, Teile, Herons; and as the Indians say, in Winter with Swans, Geese, Cranes, Duck and Mallard, and innumerable of other Water-Fowls whose names we know not which lie in the Rivers, Marshes and on the Sands: Oysters in abundance, with great store of Muscles; a sort of fair Crabs, and a round Shel-fish called Horsefeet: The Rivers stored plentifully with Fish that we saw play and leap . . . The Ayr is clear and sweet, the Country very pleasant and delightful, and we could wish, that all they that want a happy settlement, of our English Nation, were well transported thither."

In this region nature is indeed bountiful. It would seem at first glance that nobody ever had to work very hard for a living, but the short, turbulent lives of the first English settlers refute such an illusion.

The Indians, at first friendly and hospitable, gradually tired of having their property taken over and their women seduced. Other factors, including international rivalry, inter-tribal wars fomented by the English, and trade abuses, contributed to their mounting bitterness. From about 1673 to 1715 they became more and more restless until continued mistreatment at the hands of traders led to the dreadful reprisals of the

Yamasee War. It is a temptation to dwell, at this point, on the tragic story of the Red Men, so well known in outline, yet so little appreciated. But they have been gone from the Low Country for more than two hundred years. The only traces remaining of them today are the poetic names of their beloved rivers and, here and there, the piercing black eye, the straight hair and the hint of copper to be found in a few sturdy old hunters living on the edge of the swamp.

Epidemic diseases wrought terrible havoc among the colonists, particularly small-pox and yellow fever. Of the former there were severe epidemics in 1698, 1738 and 1760. Yellow fever struck in 1700, 1703, 1732, 1739, 1745 and in several later invasions.

Writing to her sister in England, Mrs. Affra Coming thus poignantly described conditions in Charles Town in 1699:

"I am sorry that I should be the messenger of so sad tidings as to desire you not to come to me till you can hear better times than here is now, for the whole country is full of trouble & sickness, 'tis the Small pox which has been mortal to all sorts of the inhabitants, especially the Indians who 'tis said to have swept away a whole neighboring nation, all to 5 or 6 which ran away and left their dead unburied, lying upon the ground for the vultures to devouer; besides the want of shipping this fall and winter & the spring is the cause of another trouble & has been followed by an earthquake & burning of the town a one third of it which they say was of equal value with what remains, besides the great loss of cattle which I know by what has been found dead of mine and being overstocked, what all these things put together makes the place look with a terrible aspect & none knows what will be the end of it."

Malaria also was a formidable scourge, especially the malignant "low country fever" which carried away so many of the youngest and best. It was well that in those early days large families were the rule. Had it been otherwise Low Country civilization, as we know it, would never have survived. In how many ancient graveyards is the mournful story told.

At an early date the settlers had learned that the white man could not survive in the lowlands during summer. This is the reason that summer villages sprang up. These were always located on high ground, generally some miles from the coast. The early pioneers knew nothing of the mosquito's rôle in the transmission of malaria, but they feared the humid "miasma" of the swamps. Luckily miasma and mosquitoes go together. In escaping one they escaped the other.

But if the white man could not live the year 'round in the swamp it was thought that the Negro could, and he was imported in large numbers. Here he increased and in a single generation became as much a part of the region as the trees of the forest. Here he developed a dialect more distinctive than any other in America, a speech which defies anyone but a native. Here he toiled as a slave but here, also, he knew a loyalty to his master and his plantation which is present to a large degree even today and which can seldom be understood by an outsider.

One fact we are prone to forget. It was his labor which made possible the golden age of the Low Country. For better or for worse our culture in South Carolina is bound up with the Negro. Its bases rest on his broad shoulders. He toiled that our fathers might cultivate literature and the arts. His women guided the first baby steps of our sires and ourselves. From him we learned the lore of the forest and the "facts of life" as well as the innumerable signs and omens presaging good luck or bad luck, fortune or death. This statement holds true for all of South Carolina except, perhaps, the mountains, but is especially applicable to the Low Country. This region has been aptly called "The Black Border" by a native who loved and interpreted the Gullah Negro probably better than anyone in his generation.

An impression exists that all of the first white settlers were English gentry. Such is far from the case. Some, it is true, were men of family and substance in the old country, but the majority were artisans, religious refugees or simply adventurers who came to the New World with the idea that they would get rich in a hurry. Many of them did—by outrageously cheating the Indians and robbing the Spaniards at St. Augustine. Perhaps the most stable early element were the Barbadians, whose way of life dominated Charles Town and much of the tidewater. They were largely of English birth or descent and had been planters in the Barbadoes. But they were not at any time in the majority. Until well into the Eighteenth Century the most numerous class was composed of English non-conformists with a sprinkling of Scotch, Irish and Dutch.

The Huguenots, who were non-conformists also, arrived in 1680 to 1685 and within half a generation had established themselves as a prosperous, stable community. With their usual arrogance the English speaking dissenters looked down on these people much as some Americans today look down on any European immigrant. The Episcopalian minority was more astute and, when the opportunity came, they took the Huguenots into their fold in a body, thus securing for themselves and their party one of the finest racial elements in America. The influence of the Huguenots in South Carolina is out of all proportion to their numbers.

By securing the Huguenot vote the High Church party was able to pass the odious acts of 1703 and 1706, establishing the Church of England as the State Church. Old enmities arising from this struggle have long been forgotten and the episode is mentioned here only because it explains how the Episcopal Church came to dominate the Low Country. The province was divided into parishes and the people were taxed to support the church. The parish registers became the bureau of vital statistics and the church wardens assumed control of all public charity. One community of New England Congregationalists moved to Georgia, but within a short time much of the best non-conformist blood was being transfused into Episcopal veins. Of course a few non-conformist churches held out, especially in Charles Town. There even one Huguenot congregation kept the old faith. Strong Baptist, Presbyterian and Congregationalist churches remained in the city and on several of the sea islands, especially Edisto.

Nevertheless, the culture which we associate with the Low Country is essentially an Episcopal culture. The urbanity, the courtesy, the worldly sophistication of the Charlestonian and the sea islander stems from his Church of England heritage, be he a Presbyterian, a Baptist or a Unitarian. Much of his gaiety and love of good living comes from the Huguenot in him. Long before the American Revolution these traits had been thoroughly fixed.

Out of this mixed group of adventurous spirits, drawn from many lands and owing allegiance to different faiths, was welded an aristocracy. It was an aristocracy not of birth but of ability. We must not forget that the Low Country, too, had its pioneer days, its Indian trade and Indian wars, its cattle industry, its battles against nature in which only the strong spirit could survive. The strong spirits did survive and in time accumulated property and wealth. The transition from log cabin to pillared mansion was swifter in the tidewater than elsewhere, but it occurred nevertheless. We forget it because it happened so long ago.

Judith Manigault, a Huguenot lady of gentle birth, left this memorial of her struggles:

"Since leaving France we have experienced every kind of affliction, disease, pestilence, famine, poverty, hard labour! I have been for six months together without tasting bread, working the ground like a slave."

In his *Life of Francis Marion* Chancellor James informs us that "men and their wives worked together in felling trees, building houses, making fences, and grubbing up their grounds, until their settlements were formed; and afterwards continued their labours at the whip-saw and in burning tar for market." In a footnote he quotes General Horry as stating that his grandfather and grandmother commenced the handsome fortune they left by working together at the whip-saw.

Having acquired lands, money and slaves the more ambitious planters set about erecting houses and churches befitting their now secure station in life. While many different styles of architecture are apparent there is one word which characterizes nearly all of their buildings—elegance. If we could go back into the past and see their log cabins, their stockade forts and their cow pens, we would realize that they had not always dwelt in mansions; but these cruder forms, being built of perishable wood and having served their purpose, are no more. We can, however, see the homes they built after they became prosperous and secure. It is these which add so much to the romance and confirm the aristocratic tradition of the Low Country.

Characteristically the early Low Country plantation home faced the river, since that was still the chief avenue of transportation and communication. The house itself, whether frame or brick, was invariably in good taste and designed to offer a commanding view from the river. The grounds were spacious. The shade trees and the avenue were generally live oak. A garden was always present, usually between the house and the river. It contained old fashioned shrubs and "exotics" such as the gardenia, the oleander, the azalea and the camellia japonica. Servants' quarters, carriage houses and stables flanked the mansion with kitchen and smokehouse closer still. From the front porch the rice fields could generally be seen, while on higher ground was grown the corn, the cotton, the indigo and the food crops.

Certainly not everybody had such a house, but this was the pattern. It was the ideal of which everybody dreamed, and it was attained by many individuals and families. It was the type of home which inevitably developed in that particular region, influenced by geography, climate and the predominant culture of the people.

Summer homes in the sand hills were not as elaborate, but were built for coolness and comfort. Here little colonies of neighbors and friends existed and for a few months each family enjoyed more intimate contacts than on the plantation.

Many planters had summer houses in the city, meaning Charleston. Here more attention was paid to elegance, since there was a great deal of entertaining. Often a planter's city home was finer than his country home. Typically most of the city homes were of the Charleston variety.

In this form of house, whether single or double, one end faces the street, a porch running lengthwise overlooks a court and catches the sea breeze, and the street door either enters the porch or opens directly into the living room.

Most of the planters' homes were of brick, although many of the earlier ones still in existence are frame. Stone, not being locally available, was seldom if ever used.

The Negro cabins were generally frame, although sometimes log. Usually the chimney was of mud, daubed on to a frame of timber. These cabins were dark and poorly ventilated, but generally clean. The yard was always carefully swept and usually some flowers were present, either old fashioned shrubs or such humbler plants as blue flags, princess feather or bouncing bet.

The dwellings of the "po' buckra" were little if any better than those of the Negroes. Drab, unpainted one- or two-room shanties in the edge of the pine woods, housing a swarm of sallow, untidy children; cotton growing up to the very front door; a razor-back hog or two in a filthy pen just outside the kitchen window. Such were the dwellings of the underprivileged, the non-slaveholding "crackers" who had had the misfortune to fall behind in the race for material success.

Volumes could be written on this class, its origins and its position in the economic and social scheme. Without attempting to offer any comprehensve explanation, my own investigation has led me to believe that in the beginning these people were of substantially the same stock as their more fortunate neighbors. Undoubtedly heredity was a factor in numerous instances, but early failure to achieve a good start was probably more frequently the reason. If a man was unable to secure slaves—the means of production— he labored under a terrific handicap, especially if living in the country. All his energies and those of his children had to be directed to getting enough to eat and clothes to wear. It is true there was game and fish aplenty, but little cash and still less credit. He therefore turned to hunting and fishing as the surest means of getting a living, perhaps working a little crop—more generally his wife and daughters working it—as a sideline.

In every land and even in the most primitive of cultures, the unlucky and the least energetic pay the penalty of being gradually shoved over into the poorest lands and humblest jobs, thus increasing their already present handicap. It is inevitable that after several generations these poor whites should emerge as a conscious group, suspicious, resentful and cunning. It is also inevitable that such a class should be looked down upon by those who were more fortunate, however charitable their intentions. One of the traits which distinguished the Low Country from the Up Country was the almost total lack of a rural middle class. In the Up Country there were yeoman farmers and small slave-holders who were ambitious and self-respecting. Below the fall-line, except perhaps west of the Edisto and in the Horry section, there were remarkably few.

We have spoken briefly of the dwelling houses but must not neglect the houses of worship. Our colonial ancestors took God very seriously and therefore much of their noblest effort was directed to the building of their churches. Low Country churches run chiefly to two architectural types, a Gothic type and a classical type, the latter resembling a Greek temple. Most of the Episcopal churches are some modification of the Gothic, though a few are massive and rectangular with heavy pillars and no steeple. This latter type is found more frequently in the non-conformist churches, although often combined with a steeple. Transitional types are to be seen and also odd little churches which defy any architectural classification. Most of the old churches have—or had—a raised pulpit and a slave gallery running around three sides. Most also had closed pews, remaining today in a few. The Church of St. James, Goose Creek, still has the royal arms of England above the pulpit.

The Negro churches, generally poor wooden structures, have a certain picturesque charm. The steeple is frequently out of proportion to the building and is often double. In Christ Church Parish most of the Negro churches have a border of "ginger cake" scrollwork under the eaves.

Of course there are no really old Negro churches, complete segregation among Christians dating no farther back than the War for Southern Independence when well meaning Northerners advised the colored brethren to form their own congregations. Prior to that time most of them were members in good standing of white churches. Indeed many of them retained their membership as long as they lived, and were buried, within this generation, from the House of God which they joined as slaves.

We have attempted to look at the tidewater region of the Low Country, knowing that this sketch is all too brief. We shall have occasion, however, to say a good deal about the middle uplands and its people, all the while remembering that it is both geographically and culturally a part of the Low Country, as much a part as the tidewater itself.

II

EXTENDING from the tidewater to the fall line is a belt roughly one hundred miles wide which for convenience I shall call the middle uplands. It is a part of the coastal plain and has every feature in common with the tidewater except those depending upon the proximity of the ocean itself. Geologically it is a part of the ancient ocean floor, and the range of hills stretching from Cheraw to Augusta are the primordial dunes where, eons ago, the waves and wind piled up mountains of white sand. These sand hills do not form a clean cut belt a few miles wide, but send spurs far down into the plain, making an irregular series of alternate ridges and valleys with here and there an isolated peak such as Sugar Loaf Mountain in Chesterfield County. As one approaches the coast, the sand hills tend to become fewer and less lofty until for the last sixty miles the belt consists of almost unbroken plain, a very few feet above sea level.

The valleys begin at the fall line and become wider toward the coast until they coalesce into a region of lush prairie interrupted by wide swamps where the rivers have eroded the soil to a depth of forty or fifty feet. Descent into these swamps is generally abrupt, the bluffs dropping in a steep angle through a subsoil of red, iron-bearing clay.

The characteristic streams of the area are dark, their amber colored water appearing black when viewed in any quantity. Typical black water streams are the Edisto, Black River, and Waccamaw.

Originating in the sand hills at or below the fall line, these streams flow through sandy or peaty soil throughout their courses. Their swamps are generally rather narrow but well timbered with cypress and gum. Some of the finest fresh water fishing in America may still be enjoyed in these beautiful streams. Bream, red breast and trout—big mouth black bass to you—are the leading items, but there are plenty of silver and calico crappie, wall-eyed pike or "jack" and channel catfish. Rock bass, while not abundant, are worth waiting for. In the spring there is the annual run of shad and, at least as far south as the Pee Dee, of herring.

Pollution is a serious problem, however, and if it is not conquered within a very short time the only fish left may be goldfish, which would, perhaps, be an example of ironic justice.

There are, of course, such large yellow streams as the Pee Dee, Santee and Savannah, originating in the Up Country and bearing their burden of clay. We are informed that before the White Man wounded his Mother Earth with the plow these yellow rivers were as clean and blue as mountain brooks. But for more than a hundred years now they have been patiently carrying away the topsoil of the Piedmont until today they have little left to transport but valueless red clay. Man, the prodigal, has all but thrown away his birthright as the dreadful problem of erosion so ably testifies.

Nature is kinder in the Low Country where the run-off is not so steep; and therefore, in spite of his stupidity, man has been unable to wreak as much havoc with the soil.

Along the rivers grow the cypress, the loblolly pine and the juniper. The swamps themselves are timbered with white oak, sweet gum, black gum, tupelo gum, cottonwood, hornbeam, hickory, ash and holly. The gordonia, or loblolly bay, and the sweet bay add beauty and fragrance.

In 1841 William Gilmore Simms, the state's foremost author, wrote to his friend William Cullen Bryant inviting him to visit Woodlands, the Simms plantation on the Edisto.

"There are no inequalities of rocks and valley in the country which we occupy," he wrote, "to strike the eye and startle the imagination, such as your native land everywhere presents,—but a mystery seems to clothe the dense and tangled masses of the forest, that lie sleeping around you. You will look, naturally, to see the brown deer emerging from the thicket; and sometimes fancy, in the flitting of some sudden shadow, that the old Indian is making his round among the graves that hide the bones of his family."

Several years ago the writer had the privilege of spending a day in one of the last tracts of virgin pine timber on the Pee Dee. It was a magnificent sight. Immense rosemary pines, averaging a hundred feet tall, stretched skyward in every direction, with groves of cypress in the sloughs. There was little undergrowth; the whole area was like a natural park where walking for miles was quite easy. Huge streamers of Spanish moss hung everywhere. It was the haunt of deer and wild turkey and man's intrusion seemed a sacrilege. This heavenly forest is now a shambles of rotting stumps, broken tops, logging roads, rusty cables and rank deciduous undergrowth. One would need an axe and a machete to penetrate a hundred yards, for what was once a cool, open grove has been converted into a sweltering jungle.

Needless to say the turkeys are gone. That proud bird would never stay in such a place, but the deer, on the other hand, will become more plentiful, since they have closer cover and protection. Perhaps in a hundred years the forest will return to something approaching its original beauty, provided it is not again sacrificed to the hungry gods of the sawmill. Or perhaps some day we will heed the voices of our far-sighted forestry experts and learn to harvest timber rather than to destroy it totally.

A feature of the middle country about which a good deal has recently been written is the bay. Characteristically the bay is a round or elliptical depression in the forest floor, generally having a small lake in the center. Surrounding each bay is a circle of dense undergrowth and vines, particularly smilax. Usually there is a low elevation of white sand around the basin, more prominent at one end. Bays are favorite homes of the bobcat, the pileated woodpecker and the timber rattlesnake. A favorite recent theory explaining these peculiar formations is that ages ago a shower of gigantic meteorites struck the earth, leaving it pock-marked over much of the southeastern United States. Certainly when viewed from the air the bays seem to form a definite sort of pattern with the deep ends all pointing in one direction. It is only fair to say, however, that this theory has not found general acceptance among scientists.

It has been noted that ridges of sand characterize the upper part of this belt. This is the region described by General Washington as "a pine barren of the worst sort." "The Road from Columbia to Camden," he said further, "goes over the most miserable pine barren I ever saw, being quite a white sand and very hilly."

Washington, the practical farmer, was thinking chiefly of the quality of the soil, as his remarks elsewhere indicate. The sand hills are indeed poor land, although with proper cultivation they will grow wonderful grapes and peaches. They can even be made fit to grow cotton and tobacco if conditioned first by planting legumes. However it is not for quality of soil that the sand hills are remarkable; it is their unique association of trees and shrubs.

The dominant tree is the long leaf pine, rivalled only by the lordly rosemary for majesty and value. These giants grow everywhere that sandy soil is to be found. Most of the old ones have been cut and they can be seen in their original beauty only in some out-of-the-way corner where one or two have escaped the lumber companies. Nearly all the remaining medium sized ones have been tapped for turpentine, but the long-leaf is a hardy organism. It can stand a forest fire better than any other tree in the South. Even the small ones nearly always survive. Where they have been cut over they will reforest themselves from the few rejected because unfit for timber. Their large, edible masts will travel for miles, blown by the winds, until finally they spiral to earth in some abandoned field. In twenty years any old field in the sand hills will be covered with young pines.

Their heart timber, from a mature tree, lasts literally forever. Many an old house built of long leaf pine a century ago is still sound and strong. Flooring ten to twelve inches wide is not uncommon in these old dwellings. The rich heart-wood from the stump makes a hot smoky fire and is wonderful kindling.

These noble trees once extended well into the Piedmont, but I do not believe there is one left above Newberry County. The last small grove that I remember seeing, near Goldville in Laurens County, has disappeared. But in the sand hills, probably because so much of the land is uncultivated, they continue to thrive in spite of man's prodigality.

Splendid efforts are now being made by the Forestry Commission to plant these and other valuable timber trees in areas unfit for agriculture. Much interest is being shown and all over the state may now be seen neat little reforestation projects, but more educational work must yet be done before a wide enough acceptance of the value of trees can be hoped for.

Closely associated with the long leaf pine are several species of small scrub oak, known collectively as "blackjack." These seldom attain a height of more than twelve or fifteen feet and are worthless as timber trees. They are good, however, for firewood, and they afford cover for wild life. In the autumn the scrub-oak woods are a riot of colors beyond the dreams of the greatest artist. Every shade of red, bronze and gold that can be imagined may be found. They are visible for miles from the crests of the long ridges.

Here and there among the black-jacks stand larger oaks, the white oak, the Southern red oak, the post oak, and several species of hickory, with sweet gum, maple and juniper in the bottoms. The naked sycamore, too, is sometimes present, lending glamor to a company of peasants.

In the spring the whole region is white with dogwood and the creek banks are pink with mountain laurel. Underneath are crow-foot violets and trailing arbutus.

Where the valleys widen into a plain the land is generally excellent and the trees are those of both the sand hills and the coast, except, however, that the liveoak tends to give place to the laurel oak, which rivals it in beauty. This lovely evergreen oak reaches its greatest abundance and finest growth in the Pee Dee section, where it is called the Darlington oak.

The middle country is the home of the partridge, the squirrel, the rabbit, the raccoon and the opossum. Deer are still fairly abundant in the big swamps and toward the coast. Turkeys are all but extinct. Bobcats lurk in the swamps and bays, but the last panther has gone the way of the bison and elk, though the panther lingered longer. There are still a few black bears, but the Santee basin was their favorite home, and since it has been flooded they will probably die out in this generation.

The middle country was opened to settlement by white people after the Yamasee War, although not many areas were actually taken up in grants until the 1730's. It was largely this area which was included in the townships as planned by Governor Robert Johnson. The first settlers were principally Scotch-Irish, Welsh and English east of the Santee, and English, Germans and Swiss to the west. Of course many families from the older settlements pushed up the rivers to join them. There are a good many Huguenot names, for example, among the early families in Darlington County. Soon there was little distinction between the different racial stocks, except that in the churches the Welsh tended to remain Baptists, the Scotch-Irish were mostly Presbyterians and the Swiss Germans below Lexington, generally forsaking the Lutheran Church, became chiefly Methodists. While there were relatively few Episcopal Churches in this section, their influence was great, since they attracted a high percentage of the leaders in each community. It may be ventured that the dominant culture of the middle country was Calvinism modified by Episcopacy. It was neither as hard and puritanical as in the Up Country nor as worldly and self-indulgent as in the tidewater.

This blended culture is naturally more pronounced near the center of the area; for example, people of Kingstree talk a good deal like Charlestonians but observe the Sabbath with Gaelic severity. In each area there is a dominant church, sometimes numerically the smallest. On the Pee Dee the Welsh Baptists were the pioneers and their descendants, now frequently Presbyterian or Episcopalian, are still powerful. The early Methodist circuit riders did their work well and large areas are dominated by the descendants of their converts. Sometimes an Episcopal Church was without a rector or a Presbyterian Church without a parson for long periods. Here the Methodists moved in. Much of the country west of the Santee must have been Lutheran in the first generation. Now there are but a handful of Lutheran churches between Lexington and Charleston Counties. This entire region is a Methodist stronghold.

Agriculture was conducted generally on a grand scale, although there were here and there a few small farmers who did all or a part of their own work. The planters cultivated large areas, chiefly in the lowlands, raising cotton and indigo. There was even some rice raised commercially along the rivers, and each plantation grew enough for its own use. A system of dykes to keep back the spring freshets was erected on the banks of the principal streams, the tree-covered remains of which may still be seen. Built by slave labor, they fell into disuse after the Confederate War and breaks were never repaired.

Dwelling houses, in general, were simpler than in the Charleston-Georgetown-Beaufort area, but were far from being cottages. Uusually they were built of heart pine on massive, hand-hewn sills and shingled with cypress. The architecture was inclined to be severe, but elaborate and pretentious homes were not uncommon. Kitchen, smoke-house, laundry, servants' quarters, carriage house and stables were grouped to the sides and rear. Avenues of Darlington oaks, cedars, sycamores or live oaks were the rule. Furniture was plain but elegant.

Every river planter of the middle uplands had his summer home in the sand hills just as was the custom in the tidewater parishes. Often the summer village was strung out for miles along the ridge above some black water stream, for example, Springville, in Darlington County. Here in the torrid summer months a boy had everything a reasonable imagination could desire. There were horses to ride, woods to walk in, fish in the creek ready to fairly jump into the frying pan. When winter came there were deer drives in the swamp; doves and partridges grew fat in every pea field; bell-tongued hounds and leaping setters strained at their leashes with the immemorial urge to hunt. Best of all, to a boy, were the 'coon hunts with the Negroes. There in the dead of night all nature seemed awful and mysterious. The weird cry of the owls, the solemn croaking of bull-frogs, the strange call of the chuckwill's-widow added an eerie charm to the black depth of the forest. One must be ever on the alert for rattlesnakes, copperheads and cotton-mouths. Besides these real dangers were a thousand imaginary ones. Jack o' lanterns were said to hover over every bog, leading the curious to some dreadful fate. Ha'nts guarded each crumbling graveyard. In the fresh-water marshes lurked the mysterious "lamprey eel, p'izen as a rattlesnake." Catamounts had been known to exert a fatal attraction by "crying like a child." Even the Devil himself had once appeared at "dese very crossroads" the time he made the bargain for Balaam Foster's soul.

The Negroes were intelligent and loyal. Of course they were not as numerous as in the Black Border, but many planters owned from fifty to a hundred. The house servants were generally of mixed blood, sometimes related to the family. They looked down on the field hands and scorned, even more, the untouchable crackers. As in the parishes, a feudal system prevailed. With all its faults this system produced leaders of men and an integrated society in which there was economic security without benefit of bureaucracy. It is of significance that the total number of lynchings in this whole area could probably be counted on the fingers of one hand. Such a record means good white people as well as good Negroes.

These Negroes are—or were—a happy people. While one would certainly not wish to turn back the clock of progress and education, it is the sad truth that the Negro of today is suffering rather acutely from growing pains. He is inclined, like the Biblical Christians, to hearken to false prophets, having itching ears. He is forsaking his 'coon hunts, his hot suppers, his protracted meetings and his fearfully and wonderfully made fraternal uniforms for less satisfying emotional outlets. He is leaving the farm in great numbers, often never to return. A mechanical cotton picker is already in production and the noise of the tractor and Deisel engine will soon drown out the last spiritual. The Negro was—and is—essentially a deserving, kind-hearted and generous soul. His faith and his loyalty often put to shame his white brother. May he find peace and happiness wherever he goes.

III

GOING from Columbia to Anderson, Greenville, Spartanburg or Rock Hill one passes through a terrain very different from that already described. There are rocks everywhere with here and there an outcropping of granite boulders. The land is no longer a plain and there are no wide swamps. Everywhere are rolling hills covered with white oak, short leaf pine and small cedars. Hickory trees are plentiful and in the valleys there are large maples and poplars. Within the lifetime of men still in their prime there were great chestnut trees, now represented by but a few naked skeletons.

The cultivated land is hilly and the serpentine rows look strange to a low countryman. Except in the valleys much of the land is frightfully eroded, though the farmers are learning at last what to do about this problem. Where erosion has been controlled the rocky soil is quite fertile, holding its moisture well and returning rich yields of corn, small grains and cotton.

The streams are swift, rocky and yellow, except the smaller creeks, which retain some of their old-time beauty and purity. Here the run-off is abrupt, making flash-floods a serious reality. The long, deep, branching valleys make the Piedmont a natural source of hydro-electric power, one of the finest anywhere in the world, and man has not failed to take advantage of this ample gift of Nature.

It must not be understood that the Up Country begins precisely where the Low Country ends. There is no smooth or clear-cut line, but a tortuously serrated zone with extensions of Spanish moss up the larger river valleys and rocky bluffs jutting down into the edge of the sand hills.

In some areas the flora is an unique combination of both Low Country and Piedmont. I know a lovely spot in upper Richland County, not far from the Fairfield line, where one can find a hillside fairly covered with glorious trillium, and where every little watercourse may be traced by the enriching purity of the swamp lily and the shooting star—not one clump, but hundreds of them. Here, under giant beeches and white oaks may be found in all their glory the dogwood, the wild azalea, the redbud and the greybeard. Here and there blossoms the elusive silver bell, a true mountain beauty, and the hearty black haw with other members of the viburnum family. Blood root and hepatica, dwarf iris and anemone nestle low among the thick carpet of fallen leaves or spring up from the crevasses of lichen-covered rocks. Acres of lush green mandrakes cover the shady margins of a meadow punctuated with perfect dwarf cedars. Overhanging the steep bluff across the garrulous little stream are gnarled old mountain laurels flanked by clumps of the wild philadelphus or syringa, while the whole area is enchanted with the fragrance of the sweet shrub. Truly an alpine community of shrubs and flowers, as different from the swamps of the Edisto as day from night; but wait! What are those broad green fronds rising above the ferns and mosses just around the bend of that tiny brook? They can't be—but they are—the farthest-flung outposts of the scrub palmetto!

Old writers tell us that this Up Country of ours was once a veritable paradise on earth. Unbroken miles of giant canebrake marked the river valleys. The forest trees were spaced far apart so that the keen-eyed hunter could see a flock of turkeys or a herd of deer as in an open park. Wide, grassy vistas relieved the monotony of the woods, covered waist high with the rich wild peavine and sustaining herds of bison. Higher in the hills ranged the elk and marauding packs of wolves sniffed silently in the swamps by day and howled eerily by night. The black bear roamed the forest unafraid and the great tawny panther crouched by the water course, awaiting his prey. Wild turkeys were everywhere, ducks and geese fed by the thousands in every lowland and flocks of wild pigeons broke the limbs of great oaks with their collective weight.

Myriads of shad and herring swam annually up the clear, blue rivers, disputing the right of way with the native bream and bass. Huge sturgeon leaped the shoals and were speared by the Indian hunters with sharp lances of fire-hardened cane. At certain places the Indians built fish dams of rock, leaving a narrow channel where their nets could be spread. Then, whooping and splashing, they would drive the fish a mile or more down-stream until enough had been collected for a whole town to give a feast.

There is one of these fish dams on Broad River, near Carlisle, remaining in a splendid state of preservation. At other times the Indians made an infusion of horse-chestnut with which they stupefied and thus captured fish in ponds or sluggish streams.

The rivers also yielded other blessings including mussels, from which the Indians secured their pearls. There were giant edible turtles; especially was one esteemed for food, the curious leatherback or soft shelled species, now becoming quite rare. Bartram was sufficiently impressed by this strange creature to make a drawing of it for his charming *Travels*. The beaver, the otter and the muskrat yielded rich furs, a fatal gift, since because of it the beaver is no more and the otter and muskrat are nearly extinct in our area.

In the northwest corner of the present state of South Carolina were the lower towns of the Cherokee Indians, perhaps the finest and most advanced native Americans north of Mexico. They embodied every trait for which the Red Man was famous, plus industry and intelligence beyond most of their race. To the east of the Cherokee, with villages on both sides of the river which bears their name, lived the Catawba people, doughty warriors and hunters, related to the intrepid Sioux of the western plains. The country between their settlements was a sort of no-man's land, though their claims overlapped and both tribes hunted between the Catawba and the Broad.

Into this productive and fascinating country about the middle of the Eighteenth Century, came the white man to fell the forest and cultivate the soil. There had, of course, been Indian traders, frontier rangers and a few hunters and squatters before this date, but 1755 marked Glen's treaty with the Cherokee Nation and the opening of the Piedmont to extensive white settlement. The Germans of Saxe Gotha and Amelia Townships were already on the frontier and quickly extended their holdings up the Broad and Saluda rivers. English and a few Huguenots from the Low Country soon followed, but the largest element to locate in the Up Country was the Scotch-Irish. Coming down from Pennsylvania and Virginia or up from Charles Town, they established focal centers throughout the Piedmont, of which the most famous were Long Canes in the west and the Waxhaws to the East.

These Scotch-Irish were, as a rule, poor but proud-spirited. They were strongly indoctrinated with certain fixed ideas, among which the superiority of the Anglo-Saxon race was rivaled in intensity only by the total depravity of man. They worshipped the Warrior God of the Old Testament and believed that scalping an Indian for bounty was just as praiseworthy as the sack of Jericho or the destruction of the Amalekites.

It might be inferred that with such harsh beliefs the Scotch-Irish had no sense of humor, but neither their stern religion nor their dangerous surroundings appear to have crushed out a certain natural light-heartedness and love of rough practical jokes. They were not permitted to dance, but all the horrors of a Covenanter's Hell could not prevent many of them from doing so, as hundreds of old church records attest. They also had a taste for hard cider and mountain dew. Their parties were hilarious and every wedding furnished an opportunity to serenade the embarrassed young couple with loud music and broad humor. For those who dared not dance there were play-party games where holding hands or kissing was in order. And everywhere the fiddler, the banjo picker and the ballad singer were welcome guests.

Perhaps some of this love of fun and good living may have come from Irish blood, for contrary to oft-repeated statements these people were not merely Scotch who had sojourned for a few generations in Ireland.

From the *Heads of Families, First Census of the United States*, taken in 1790, we glean the following "native" Irish names among the "Scotch-Irish" of Fairfield, Chester, Lancaster, York, Abbeville, Edgefield, Greenville, Laurens, Newberry, Pendleton, Spartanburg, and Union districts: Shane, Kilpatrick, Kennedy, Duggans, Cork, Murphy, Kearnaghan, Roney, Collins, Dougherty, Dennis, Clenighan, Milligan, Shannon, O'Mullin, Kelley, Millington, Sullivan, Merony, Gillihan, Ussery, Lafferty, Mahaffy, Mulligan, O'Berry, O'Conner, Dunnahoo (sic), Connelly, Flannegan, O'Neal, Dempsey, O'Shields, Casey and Hogan. Many of these recur dozens of times, especially Kelley, Kennedy and Kilpatrick. Although it is tempting to include other suggestive names such as McCluskey, McCaskey and McConnell, no names beginning with "Mc" or "Mac" are offered as evidence, since it might be argued that they were originally Scotch. While a portion of these names may have belonged to actual Irish immigrants who came up from Charles Town, so many of them have been traditionally Presbyterian as strongly to suggest their presence among the original Scotch-Irish settlers. The writer attended Presbyterian College in Clinton, where practically the entire student body came from this racial stock and among the names enrolled were Dulin, Dugan, Flannigan, Ussery, Kennedy, O'Daniel, Murphy, Clowney, Carrigan and a host of "Mc's."

These Scotch-Irish were not only dominant numerically, but their culture set the pattern for the entire section. Their religion was Presbyterian, which meant that they believed in complete democracy of government and an independent clergy. They also believed in education, and such as was obtainable in the backwoods came from the "Irish schoolmaster" with his well-worn bundle of birch switches. They were willing to bow to God, but not to any man on earth. In frontier warfare they were in the habit of arguing with their officers or actually disobeying them if they chose. They fought Indians almost continually, but adopted many of their habits, particularly their methods on the war path. In their belts they carried a tomahawk and a scalping knife and there is plenty of evidence to prove that they used both weapons frequently and effectively.

Their agile feet were often shod with deerskin moccasins and they shot the awkward frontier rifle with deadly accuracy.

Their leaders were well-educated men, especially their pastors, who were almost invariably on the side of the revolutionary movement when that momentous issue arose.

In 1760 their country was the West, and like that of a later day was complete with cattle ranches called cow pens, horse thieves, claim jumpers and renegades who liked nothing better than murdering an Indian trapper for his pelts. If such an incident brought on an Indian war, it made little difference to the perpetrators. Most of the settlers, however, were honest men and women who were grateful to God for a few acres of land, a simple cabin built of hand-hewn logs, abundant game and freedom under an open sky. At first their settlements were compact, generally along the rivers, with here and there a stockade fort built for protection against the Red Man.

It is but natural that their homes were simpler and their wants fewer than their neighbors nearer the coast. After all, the planters of the tidewater had a start of seventy-five years. The backwoodsmen of the Piedmont scorned the soft life they pictured these aristocrats as leading. They also distrusted the dominant religion of the Low Country as smacking of "popery."

Doubtless there was more than a trace of unconscious envy in their feelings, too, since as soon as they became prosperous, they bought Negroes and built finer homes for themselves. Early in the Nineteenth Century the culture of cotton displaced indigo and cattle raising in the Up Country, and with cotton the picture changed. Several areas took on a distinctly Low Country flavor, particularly Fairfield, the only Piedmont county with a Negro majority. In this and similar areas the plantations tended to become larger and the homes more pretentious. Low Country planters themselves moved in considerable numbers up into the hills, bringing with them their slaves. There were several reasons for this tendency; the Up Country was healthier; there was more available land; many of the large Low Country estates had been so divided by inheritance that a young man had little left at home.

Nevertheless the tone of the Up Country remained singularly democratic. True, there were many "great families," looked up to and respected by all, but the "judge" or the "colonel" could always be met on terms of easy familiarity. Often he had relatives who were one-horse farmers and lacked the advantages of education. Today this tendency persists. In an Up Country town the mill owner is quite likely to employ a cousin or two as weavers or doffers. The local dowager, whose proudest distinction is that she is Regent of the D.A.R., will share the same storied ancestor with the village dressmaker.

Here, unlike the Low Country, there was, and is, a middle class. No rigid line ever divided one group from another, the transition being so gradual that often it is impossible to determine.

In the Up Country there were never as many Negroes, except in the few localities above mentioned. A man owning as many as thirty or forty slaves was accounted a big planter; one with a hundred was a nabob. The average slaveholding family owned perhaps from six to eight, many but one or two. Those who owned none resented the institution of slavery. When the Negroes were freed they thought of them as competitors in the field of labor and their resentment became even more bitter than during slavery times. It is this feeling, along with other factors, which has produced the spectacle of lynchings.

Religion, under whatever label, is strongly Calvinistic in the Up Country. Hellfire and damnation are still preached in terms as strong as those used by Jonathan Edwards or Cotton Mather. Revival meetings occur annually, even in the larger cities, where sinners are brought weeping to the altar. It is still felt that every Christian must have a conviction of utter depravity and guilt before he can become a child of God.

But, if the Up Countryman rejoices in his total depravity he also insists on his free will and it is often remarkably free. He is fiercely independent and resents anyone, with the possible exception of the preacher, telling him what to do. Free advice and criticism from outsiders is especially objectionable. When strangers, particularly Federal revenue officers, go probing about his creek bottom, he has been known to express his distaste by shooting the intruders.

Baptists and Methodists now greatly outnumber the Presbyterians in the Up Country, though the latter, including the A. R. P.'s, still set the cultural tone in such counties as Fairfield, Chester, York and Abbeville. Just as the numerically small Episcopal Church has dominated the tidewater, so the Presbyterian Church has held much the same position in the Piedmont. It is the church of most of the "old families," even if many of their descendants have gone elsewhere. The Presbyterians, insisting on an educated ministry, lost thousands of members in the decades immediately following the American Revolution. There were simply not enough Presbyterian preachers to go around. On the other hand, a Methodist or Baptist with a strong sense of being "called" could bring his fervent eloquence to bear on many a congregation without a shepherd. His illustrations might be homely and his grammar a trifle uncertain, but often he could arouse the people much more successfully than could his more scholarly brother.

Every major Protestant denomination in South Carolina except the Episcopalians has one or more colleges. The total is now ten. Prior to recent consolidations due to financial difficulties there were nearly twice as many. The Scotch-Irish have always been credited with a zeal for education, and it may be significant that of these institutions one is in Columbia, one in Hartsville and all the rest in the Piedmont.

The soul of a region is often best expressed in its buildings, particularly its dwelling houses and its churches. The typical ante-bellum Up Country plantation house is as Scotch-Irish as the rugged old farmer who built it. Its straight, uncompromising lines suggest a rigid conscience, its lasting timbers and sturdy workmanship a sense of appreciation for the worthwhile things of life. That shaded well, curbed with boulders of rough granite, brings to mind the fountain of living waters which may be sought beneath the shadow of a great Rock, in a weary land.

The first dwellings were, of course, built of logs, but with the advent of prosperity frame houses became the rule. Some of the earliest of these had a "dog run" through the middle, for coolness. This was a central open hallway, leading from front to rear with no doors to prevent the breezes from passing through. This was wonderfully cool in summer. Most of these old houses are gone, but they seem to have followed the frontier as it moved west, and are therefore still fairly plentiful in western Georgia, Alabama, Tennessee and Arkansas.

Of the houses still standing which are a century or more old, the best known type is the two-storied frame house with a porch running across the front and an "l" to the rear. Unlike the early Low Country houses, which faced the river, the Up Country house faced the road. There was generally less of an avenue present than in the Low Country, except where the influence of that section had crept in. The front yard was usually fenced and a small shrub garden concealed the portion below the first floor. Generally there was no basement except perhaps a small cellar to the rear. As in the Low Country the kitchen of the more pretentious dwellings was in a separate building. Servants' houses, carriage-houses and stables were in the back yard and the slave quarters were a short distance across the fields. The big house was of heart pine timber, generally fastened together with hand-made wrought iron nails, or, in some of the oldest houses, wooden pegs.

The humbler houses were put together in much the same way, but were smaller and less elaborate. Generally the cooking here was done in the big stone chimney of the living room, which served as kitchen and dining room as well. Baking was often done in dome-shaped outdoor ovens, particularly in the German settlements.

Churches, like the houses, had more of rectitude and less of grace. They were, as a rule, rectangular in ground plan and some had a single tall steeple on the front. A few here and there followed the Greek classical style with massive columns and a low-pitched roof. Gothic architecture was seldom seen except among the Episcopal churches. Nearly all of the older churches had a gallery for the slaves, although some of these were taken out long ago. Although most of the old Up Country churches were of frame construction a few were of stone or brick. These were scarcely more elaborate, however, than those of wood.

The Up Country began as a frontier and its people, its speech and its institutions still reflect a little of the frontier influence despite the fact that civilization here is nearly two hundred years of age. Though land was plentiful and game abundant, life was far from easy for the first fifty years. The restless spirit of the pioneer, which prompted him to conquer this wilderness, also prompted many of his sons to move on. You can find them in Tennessee, in Alabama, in Arkansas and in Texas. Three of them were among the leaders who fell at the Alamo. They have gone far and wide, but most often they have gone westward. Whenever you find one you will know you have met a proud and independent spirit, part fatalist, part anarchist and something of a mystic.

The Up Country seems to be entering upon a new era, the age of industry. Even its agriculture is taking on a new vigor and once more there is stock raising on a fairly large scale. Its hills are covered with the beautiful orchards which have made South Carolina the leading peach-growing state of the nation. Though many of its fields are eroded and its timber sadly mismanaged, there is power in its swift streams and energy in its people. As in its infancy, the Up Country is still a land of opportunity for those who are not afraid of work.

IV

THERE is just a fringe of true mountains in South Carolina, but they are among the most beautiful to be found anywhere in America. Old James Adair, the Indian trader and scholar, compared them favorably with the Alps. Catesby hunted buffalo among them and Bartram grew eloquent when he spoke of the vale of Keowee.

In colonial times these great forested hills were rightfully called the Cherokee Mountains, and should still be so named, since no Apalachee Indians ever lived there. They were the home of the Cherokee at least from the time of DeSoto and probably from pre-Columbian days. The lower towns of that people were located in the present counties of Oconee and Pickens, with a few in adjacent parts of North Carolina and Georgia. Here some of the most colorful colonial and Revolutionary history was enacted and here, when the Indians had departed, settled the hardiest and most fiercely independent of the Up Countrymen.

South Carolina's mountains are a part of the Blue Ridge and are most prominent in Oconee, Pickens, Greenville and Spartanburg Counties, where they border on the Georgia and North Carolina lines. There are several peaks of considerable height, notably Mt. Pinnacle and Table Rock. Caesar's Head, named for an almost forgotten Cherokee chief, bears a fancied resemblance to a rudely sculptured head. There are dozens of lovely waterfalls, the most notable of which is Whitewater. Sheer cliffs of granite hundreds of feet high are frequent, as at Caesar's Head and Table Rock Mountain.

It is the flora, however, which makes the mountains so interesting. The trees, shrubs and flowering plants are those of New England rather than of the deep South. Before the lamented chestnut blight filled the forest with pale, dry skeletons, every acre of mountainside was virtually a chestnut grove. The white oak, the chestnut oak and the hickory are everywhere. The walnut family is represented by the butternut, a typical New England tree. The sugar maple is also present, although we do not take advantage of it as Adair informs us the Indians did. Several species of rhododendron make the mountainside a gorgeous spectacle in the spring and early summer and this beauty is intensified by the mountain laurel, the leucothoe and the native azalea. Here the silver-bell becomes a veritable tree in size, rather than a mere shrub. Here are greybeard and buckeye and many lush green vines, of which several species of wild grape are perhaps the most abundant. Blueberries in profusion may be picked in the open woods and, although the chestnuts are gone, chinquapins still are plentiful.

The wild life of the mountains differs little from that of the Piedmont except that species are preserved which have become extinct farther down the state. There are a few deer and perhaps an occasional black bear, both of these species being abundant in the Great Smokies of North Carolina and Tennessee. The hedgehog or woodchuck is found in the South Carolina mountains and the game laws still provide a season for the shooting of the ruffed grouse. Rainbow and speckled trout are fairly plentiful in the cold clear streams and catfish grow to a considerable size.

The mountain people are essentially the same as those who settled the Up Country in general. Perhaps, however, there is a higher percentage of "pure" Scotch-Irish and English with less of German or other strains. The mountaineer is traditionally conservative and has been aptly described as "our contemporary ancestor." All the old colonial handicrafts survived until a few years ago, including spinning, hand weaving and iron working. The mountaineer still has his dried herbs hanging in bunches from rafters and his festoons of bright red peppers. On his bed there usually is a patchwork quilt, and a hooked rug lies in front of his door. And there may possibly be an old mountain rifle, long, heavy and muzzle-loading, over his chimney. He'll not be using it any more, but it is a proud heirloom of the long ago.

Mountain houses are, in general, less pretentious than those in the Piedmont. The average mountain dwelling is a one-story cottage, sometimes quite picturesque, but as often bare and unattractive. There are still a good many log cabins remaining in the mountains, probably more than in any other section. The house is generally built not far from a spring, but if it is in a valley there is likely to be a deep well of clear, cold water. Outhouses are few, perhaps a stable, a corn crib and smokehouse. As in the Low Country there may be a pole with a half dozen dried gourds for the purple martins. This is an old trait, taken, like many another, directly from the Indians.

The mountain farmer cultivates corn, which he considers it his right to dispose of as he pleases, vegetables, and a little patch of tobacco. The latter is entirely for his own use. He cures it not by artificial heat, as in the Pee Dee section, but by drying under a shed. He then rolls the leaves up into a twist, which may be either chewed or smoked.

There is little money to be made by farming in the mountains, except in the rich valley areas. For this reason a great many mountain families have moved into the textile centers and have entered industry. They form a considerable proportion of textile operatives through the Southeast.

Because of the pitiful returns from agriculture, there being almost no money crop, many mountain farmers have long been in the habit of converting their corn into whiskey. This they do in small, home-constructed stills, hidden far from the travelled highways. During the prohibition era their product found a ready sale and many of the more enterprising enjoyed real prosperity, though at the risk of arrest and a Federal sentence. The industry has declined, however, since the advent of legal whiskey.

Slowly the mountaineer is being educated, industrialized and cut to the general American standard. His lovely old ballads are being replaced by synthetic "Hill Billy" songs, dreary, monotonous and artificial. The old fiddler or banjo picker is being crowded out by the ubiquitous radio. Only the hills remain as once they were.

PLATES

May River, near Bluffton

I

THE CARD HOUSE, BLUFFTON. *Ante Bellum*

Street in Bluffton

White Church, St. Helena Island. *c. 1725*   IV

Seagull Sandspit, near Hunting Island   V

Crofut House, Beaufort. *c. 1855*

VI

Prince William's Church, Sheldon. *1753*

VII

LEA HOUSE, BEAUFORT. *Pre-Revolutionary*   VIII

Live Oak Avenue, Tomotley   IX

STREET IN ROCKVILLE

Palmettos, Edisto Island

Edisto Presbyterian Church. *1831*   XII

Marsh Scene on the Edisto   XIII

SLAVE CABIN, JOHN'S ISLAND   XIV

CHURCH STREET AT TRADD, CHARLESTON   XV

MILES BREWTON HOUSE, CHARLESTON. *c. 1769*

XVI

PIRATE HOUSE, CHARLESTON. *Pre-Revolutionary* XVII

St. Philip's, Charleston. *1838*   XVIII

ROPER HOUSE, CHARLESTON. *c. 1850*

Rainbow Row, Charleston

Live Oaks, Mepkin Plantation   XXI

WALKWAY, MAGNOLIA ON THE ASHLEY   XXII

REFLECTION POOL, MAGNOLIA GARDENS   XXIII

The Mulberry, on Cooper River. *1714*

XXIV

Strawberry Chapel, Childsbury. *1725*

XXV

Middleton Place Gardens

XXVI

Dukes House, Summerville. *c. 1835*

RUINS OF DORCHESTER FORT. *1775*

XXVIII

CYPRESS GARDENS   XXIX

Masonic Temple, Georgetown. *1735*   XXX

Prince George's, Winyah, Georgetown. *1742*

XXXI

COLLETON COUNTY COURTHOUSE, WALTERBORO. *1822*

BLACK RIVER, NEAR KINGSTREE   XXXIII

Swimming Hole, Black River   XXXIV

Carolina Hall, near Mars Bluff. *c. 1850*   XXXV

HART HOUSE, HARTSVILLE. *1817*

CYPRESS POND, LEE COUNTY   XXXVII

McLendon House, Bishopville. *Ante Bellum*   XXXVIII

SALEM CHURCH, BLACK RIVER. *1846*   XXXIX

Swamp Scene, near Eutaw Springs

XL

St. David's Episcopal Church, Cheraw. *1773*   XLI

Borough House, Stateburg. *1754*   XLII

Swan Lake Gardens, Sumter   XLIII

CHURCH OF THE HOLY CROSS, STATEBURG. *1850*   XLIV

Detail of Doorway, Church of the Holy Cross   XLV

Dunndell Gardens, near Stateburg

XLVI

Negro Cabin, Barnwell County

XLVII

Andrew Pickens House, Edgefield, *c. 1816*

GOVERNOR'S MANSION, COLUMBIA. *1855*   XLIX

SOUTH CAROLINIANA LIBRARY, COLUMBIA. *1840*

Trinity Episcopal Church, Columbia. *1847*

Seibels House, Columbia. *c. 1787*

First Presbyterian Church, Columbia. *1853*

RUINS OF MILLWOOD, COLUMBIA. *Prior to 1820*   LIV

Peavine Hayfield, Richland County

LV

MULBERRY PLANTATION, NEAR CAMDEN. *1820*

Side View, Mulberry Plantation House

Bethesda Presbyterian Church, Camden. *1820*

LVIII

REAR VIEW, BETHESDA   LIX

Burt House, Abbeville. *c. 1850*

Brice House, Winnsboro. *c. 1835*   LXI

PRESBYTERIAN CHURCH, COKESBURY. *1883*   LXII

Masonic Female College, Cokesbury. *1856*

Mᴛ. Mᴏʀɪᴀʜ Bᴀᴘᴛɪsᴛ Cʜᴜʀᴄʜ, ɴᴇᴀʀ Gʀᴇᴇɴᴡᴏᴏᴅ. *1835*

LXIV

Stony Point, near Greenwood. *1825*   LXV

House at Musgrove's Mill. *Pre-Revolutionary*

LXVI

Negro Cabin, Laurens County   LXVII

Culp House, Union. *c. 1857*

LXVIII

Congress Street, York

LXIX

LAND'S FORD LOCKS, CHESTER COUNTY. *1823*

Foster's Tavern, Spartanburg. *c. 1807*

Administration Building, Cedar Springs. *1860*

Shiloh Methodist Church, near Inman. *c. 1825*   LXXIII

Zimmerman House, Glenn Springs. *1852*   LXXIV

SALUDA RIVER SCENE, GREENVILLE COUNTY

LXXV

Poinsett Bridge, Greenville County. *1820*

LXXVI

Detail of Arch, Poinsett Bridge

LXXVII

CAESAR'S HEAD

LXXVIII

LITTLE RIVER, OCONEE

Horseshoe Robinson's House, Oconee. *Prior to 1800*

Old Stone Church, near Pendleton. *1802*

Farmers' Society Building, Pendleton. *1828*

Fort Hill, Clemson. *c. 1807*   LXXXIII

OCONEE STATION GUARDHOUSE. *1760*

DETAIL OF BACK ENTRANCE, OCONEE STATION　　　　　LXXXV

WILLIAM RICHARDS HOUSE, OCONEE. *1805*

LXXXVI

SAM BIBLE'S MILL, PICKENS COUNTY   LXXXVII

Isaqueena Falls, Oconee Creek

LXXXVIII

TABLE ROCK MOUNTAIN   LXXXIX

NOTES ON PLATES

FRONTISPIECE

CHURCH OF THE HOLY TRINITY, Grahamville. Jasper County. 1860. In the late 1820's, Grahamville became a popular summer resort village with numbers sufficient to justify the formation of a separate congregation. Prior to that time, communicants from upper St. Luke's parish made a lengthy and arduous carriage journey to St. Luke's Church near Prichardville. In 1830 a modest frame chapel was erected on lands donated by William Heyward. The present house of worship, a gift of James Bolan, was consecrated just before the outbreak of the Confederate War. Because it was used as Federal headquarters, it escaped the torch of the Union army which destroyed the rectory and a number of other beautiful homes and buildings in St. Luke's parish.

PLATE II

THE CARD HOUSE, Bluffton. Beaufort County. Ante Bellum. This typical Low Country cottage, called "the Card House" because of its construction, is built to catch the breezes from all directions. It faces the May River. According to Miss Agnes Coe, Bluffton's oldest inhabitant, now 94, this cottage was standing when she was a child, owned then by the Graham family. The property was part of the original Pope tract. The present owner is Miss Harriet R. Colquitt.

PLATE IV

WHITE CHURCH, St. Helena Island. Beaufort County. c. 1725. Constructed as a Chapel of Ease to the St. Helena's parish church in Beaufort, this tabby building was destroyed by a forest fire about 1865. The exact date of construction is unknown but it was probably built about the same time as St. Helena's, constructed in 1724.

PLATE VI

CROFUT HOUSE, Beaufort. c. 1855. Built of brick in variegated colors as a residence for Dr. Barnwell Sams, the Crofut house was used as a hospital during the Confederate War. The two-story portico is topped by a flat roof rather than the customary pediment. In the rear are a picturesque tabby kitchen and servants' quarters opening into a court. The present owners are Mrs. George Waterhouse and Miss Rita Crofut.

PLATE VII

PRINCE WILLIAM'S CHURCH, near Sheldon. Beaufort County. 1753. Prince William's parish was established in 1745 and eight years later the wealthy planters of the vicinity constructed one of the most impressive houses of worship in the province. It was built on glebe lands donated by Elizabeth Bellinger, widow of the second Landgrave Edmund Bellinger. A leaden equestrian statue of Prince William, Duke of Cumberland, which stood in the church yard, was torn down and melted into bullets for

the American Army. The church was burned by the British troops of General Augustine Prévost who besieged Charles Town in 1779. In 1826, using the original three-and-one-half foot walls of English bond, the church was rebuilt only to be burned again by Sherman's 15th Corps under General John A. Logan. Annually, on the Sunday after Easter, a memorial service is conducted here by the bishop and clergy of the diocese.

PLATE VIII

LEA HOUSE, Beaufort. Pre-Revolutionary. Originally a Jenkins plantation home on St. Helena Island, the Lea House was purchased and moved to Beaufort by a member of the Rhett family. The present owner is Mrs. Clyde Wheeler, daughter of the late Peter L. Lea.

PLATE IX

LIVE OAK AVENUE, Tomotley. Beaufort County. Patience Izard, wife of Abraham Eustis and last Izard owner of Tomotley, began planting the four spectacular live oak avenues which radiate from the site of the plantation house about 1820. Tomotley was part of 48,000 acres granted to Capt. Edmund Bellinger, who was made a landgrave in 1698. It is owned now by the Thorne family.

PLATE XII

EDISTO PRESBYTERIAN CHURCH, Edisto Island. Charleston County. 1831. Scotch Presbyterians are believed to have organized a church on Edisto Island between 1680 and 1710. In 1705 Henry Bower obtained a grant of 300 acres from the lords proprietors which he conveyed in trust for the use of the Presbyterian minister on Edisto Island. Several years later the church received a donation of slaves to work on these lands. The present structure was built in 1831 from designs attributed to James M. Curtis of Charleston.

PLATE XVI

MILES BREWTON HOUSE, 27 King Street, Charleston. c. 1769. One of the best examples of the Georgian type residence in Charleston, the Miles Brewton house was headquarters for Sir Henry Clinton and Lord Rawdon during the British occupation and again in 1865 for Federal troops. Ezra Waite executed the elaborate and elegant woodcarvings and may possibly have been the architect. The Brewton family was lost at sea in 1775, the house being left to Miles Brewton's sister, Mrs. Rebecca Motte. Miss Susan P. Frost, the present owner, is a lineal descendant of Mrs. Motte.

PLATE XVII

"PIRATE HOUSE," 145 Church Street, Charleston. Pre-Revolutionary. Although there isn't a vestige of historical proof, tradition holds that this house was used by early

18th century pirates who harassed the South Carolina coast. A fine example of French village architecture, with tinted stucco walls and a red tile roof, the Pirate House is believed to have been built by a Huguenot family. Its present owner is Robert A. Talbot.

PLATE XVIII

ST. PHILIP'S, 146 Church Street, Charleston. 1838. Erected from plans by Joseph Hyde on the site of an older church which was destroyed by fire, this house of worship serves the oldest Anglican parish south of Virginia. The impressive octagonal steeple, designed by Edward Brickell White, was added in 1848.

PLATE XIX

ROPER HOUSE, No. 9 East Battery, Charleston. c. 1850. Edward Benjamin Bryan is thought to have been the architect of this typical ante bellum town house. The first owner was William Roper whose sister, Julia Grace Roper, married Bryan in 1849. It is now owned by S. R. Guggenheim.

PLATE XXI

LIVE OAKS, Mepkin Plantation, Charleston County. Situated 29 miles above Charleston on the western branch of the Cooper River, Mepkin was purchased in 1762 by Henry Laurens, distinguished Charleston merchant and president of the Continental Congress. The original gates and avenues are intact but a new residence stands on the site of the first plantation house. The present owners are Henry and Clare Booth Luce.

PLATES XXII AND XXIII

MAGNOLIA GARDENS, Charleston County. Thomas Drayton emigrated from Barbados in 1671. About 1700 he acquired a part of the lands now embraced in Magnolia on the Ashley River and laid out a stately English park. One of his descendants, the Rev. John Grimké Drayton, advised by his physicians to stay in the open as much as possible, developed the park into a natural, informal type of garden, now a world-famous beauty spot. C. Norwood Hastie, grandson of the Reverend Mr. Drayton, is the present owner. The original colonial dwelling was destroyed by Union soldiers in 1865.

PLATE XXIV

THE MULBERRY, Berkeley County. 1714. Popularly known as "Mulberry Castle," this elaborate Jacobean baroque dwelling was called The Mulberry by its builder, Thomas Broughton, because of a great mulberry tree on the plantation. An ancient mulberry grove stands on the south lawn. Broughton, a colonial planter, soldier and Indian trader, is said to have modeled his house after the seat of his family at Seaton, England. During the Yamasee War, The Mulberry became a fortified refuge. Loopholes for muskets pierce the heavy oak shutters and walls, and trapdoors in the floor of the square flanking towers lead to small cellars where ammunition was stored. The house stands on a bluff, once known as Mulberry Landing, overlooking the Cooper River. Lawrence Walker of Summerville is the present owner.

PLATE XXV

STRAWBERRY CHAPEL, Childsbury. Berkeley County. 1725. In 1723 an Act of Assembly authorized the establishment of a parochial Chapel of Ease for the convenience of parishioners living at a distance from Biggin Church. This chapel had parochial rights of baptism and burial but neither rectory nor endowment. Situated on the western branch of the Cooper River at the north side of Strawberry ferry, the chapel was part of a proposed community named Childsbury for James Child, its founder and promoter. Child's will provided for a free school, a "university," a house for the minister, and an acre and a half of land for the church. The free school existed for many years but today all that remains of the community is the chapel which borrowed the name of the nearby ferry.

PLATE XXVI

MIDDLETON PLACE GARDENS, Dorchester County. In 1740 Henry Middleton, later temporary president of the first Continental Congress, sent to England for a landscape gardener. A hundred slaves are said to have worked ten years to lay out the formal pattern of walks, terraces and flower beds. The French botanist, André Michaux, in 1785 introduced a number of exotic plants which spread from Middleton Place to all parts of the country. Arthur Middleton, who signed the Declaration of Independence, added to the gardens. The manor house, built in the middle of the 19th century, was burned by Federal soldiers. J. J. Pringle Smith is the present owner.

PLATE XXVII

DUKES HOUSE, Summerville. Dorchester County. c. 1835. Style, materials, workmanship and tradition indicate that this residence was built some time between 1830 and 1840. The original owner was John R. Dukes. The present owner is Mrs. George S. Weed.

PLATE XXVIII

RUINS OF DORCHESTER FORT. Dorchester County. 1775. This fort is popularly believed to have been constructed in the early days of the Congregationalist village of Dorchester, which was planted on the left bank of the Ashley in 1696, but such is not the case. These well-preserved tabby walls are almost certainly those of a Revolutionary fort constructed in 1775 by order of the Council of Safety.

PLATE XXIX

CYPRESS GARDENS, Dean Hall Plantation. Berkeley County. Created from swamp lands and rice-reserve waters, Cypress Gardens on the Cooper River are new gardens in an old and beautiful setting. They are characterized by black lagoons and winding waterways, shaded with moss-draped cypress and gum and brightened by spots of color from blooming daffodils, iris and azaleas. Benjamin Kitteredge is the owner and creator.

PLATE XXX

MASONIC TEMPLE, Georgetown. 1735. Constructed of materials brought from England, this stuccoed brick building, painted white to resemble stone, has served as a bank, armory, hotel and meeting hall. Its square, massive structure suggests a fort. A bronze marker on the wall states that it housed the "first and only colonial bank in the colonies," a claim which is not supported by historical evidence.

PLATE XXXI

PRINCE GEORGE'S, WINYAH. Georgetown. 1742. This venerable church serves a parish founded in 1721. It was constructed with funds derived in part from a special temporary tax on imported liquors. The building materials, except for oyster shell cement which was made on the spot, were imported from England. The clock tower was added in 1820. During the British occupation of Georgetown the interior was burned. The flagstone floor bears marks which tradition holds were made by the British horses which were stabled here.

PLATE XXXII

COLLETON COUNTY COURTHOUSE, Walterboro. 1822. Built by Col. W. N. Thompson and designed, at least in part, by Robert Mills, this plain Greek Revival structure rests on an arcaded basement. The portico, with its four unfluted Doric columns, is flanked by curved stairs. The courthouse was authorized by the General Assembly in 1817 and although the date incised in the pediment indicates it was built in 1820, it is doubtful that it was completed until a year or two later because of difficulties in clearing the title to the land and alterations in the design. In 1828 the first public Nullification meeting in South Carolina was held here. The wings were added in 1939.

PLATE XXXV

CAROLINA HALL, near Mars Bluff. Florence County. c. 1850. This white frame Greek Revival plantation dwelling with its twenty-two free standing columns was built by Dr. William R. Johnson in the "golden years" just before the Confederate War. Its windows are square-headed and its entrance has side lights and a transom. The present owners are Mr. and Mrs. B. H. Harwell.

PLATE XXXVI

HART HOUSE, Hartsville. Darlington County. 1817. Thomas and Hannah Coker Hart built this simple plantation dwelling. Mrs. David R. Coker, its present owner, has developed here a private garden of rare charm and beauty. An unusual topographic situation, caused by the vigorous action of a nearby stream, has resulted in an exotic amalgam of hills, ravines and swamps where the flora of both mountains and lowlands flourishes. Untold years ago, Black Creek, which rises in the Piedmont of North Carolina and empties into the Pee Dee River, brought down the seeds of the *Kalmia latifolia*, or mountain laurel. From this alpine plant Kalmia Gardens takes its name.

PLATE XXXVIII

McLENDON HOUSE, Bishopville. Lee County. 1815-1845. The one-story rear portion of this residence is shown on a map made by S. H. Boykin, surveyor, in 1821 as the home of A. Dixon. The two-story front portion was added about 1845 by Charles Spencer. The present owners are Mr. and Mrs. R. Eugene McLendon.

PLATE XXXIX

SALEM PRESBYTERIAN CHURCH, Black River. Sumter County. 1846. The first church on this site was a log cabin meeting house built in 1759. It was replaced about a decade later by a frame building. In 1804 a brick house of worship was constructed. The present edifice was built in 1846. The congregation itself was formed between 1737 and 1739.

PLATE XLI

ST. DAVID'S EPISCOPAL CHURCH, Cheraw. Chesterfield County. 1773. Situated in an area colonized by Welsh settlers before the Revolutionary War, this church was named for the patron saint of Wales. The 71st Scotch Regiment of Cornwallis' army used the building as a hospital during a smallpox epidemic and a number of British soldiers who fell victim to this disease are buried in the old cemetery. St. David's became a hospital for the second time during the Confederate War and "blood stains" are said to be still visible on the boards beneath the carpeted floor. The parish was established in 1768.

PLATE XLII

BOROUGH HOUSE, Stateburg. Sumter County. 1754. Thomas and Mary Hooper purchased and developed this place some years prior to the Revolution, and their descendants have maintained it through all the history-packed years since. The original owner was William Hilton, to whom the property was granted in 1754. In 1821, Dr. William Wallace Anderson, a distinguished surgeon and amateur architect who had married a daughter of the house, re-designed the building as it now stands. The central portion was left intact but two small wings were replaced by flanking additions of *pisé de terre* or rammed earth. The separate library building, kitchen, servants' house and other outbuildings are also of *pisé de terre*. The Borough House derives its name from having been the principal residence of the old village of Stateburg(h), colloquially known as "the borough." The doors of the central hall are branded with "C. A." a memento from General Greene's Continental Army which used the dwelling for its headquarters. Lord Cornwallis also occupied the Borough House. The present owner is Mrs. Walter C. White, whose family has occupied Borough House for eight generations.

PLATE XLIII

SWAN LAKE GARDENS, Sumter. H. C. Bland of Sumter has converted a swampy lowland on the outskirts of the city into an exquisite show-place. Rare Japanese iris with their brilliant hues border a lake dotted with pink and white pond lilies. The black and white swans, which glide gracefully among tiny islands shaded by willow and cypress, give the gardens their name.

PLATES XLIV AND XLV

CHURCH OF THE HOLY CROSS, Stateburg. Sumter County. 1850. This notable example of Gothic Revival architecture is constructed of *pisé de terre*—earth packed between wooden molds, tamped, and left to dry until it became as hard as baked brick. For almost a century, it has withstood heat, cold, storms and even an earthquake. The interior of the building has tiled floors, carved walnut woodwork and handsome stained glass windows. It is covered by a red tile roof. The architect was Edward C. Jones of Charleston. The present building is the second on the site, replacing a frame building constructed when Claremont Parish was incorporated in 1788. The name of the Parish was changed when the new church was built.

PLATE XLVI

DUNNDELL GARDENS, near Stateburg. Sumter County. A historic mill pond which has been in existence for more than a century and a half is the setting for Dunndell Gardens. This site, in the High Hills of the Santee, was the home place of Chancellor Thomas Waites, an eminent South Carolina jurist and Revolutionary soldier. Virtually every known variety of iris blooms among an intricate pattern of spring-fed creeks and ponds. Dr. J. Ralph Dunn is the owner.

PLATE XLVIII

ANDREW PICKENS HOUSE, Edgefield. c. 1816. Governor Andrew Pickens, son of the Revolutionary general and father of Francis W. Pickens, South Carolina's first Confederate governor, built this dwelling, known as Halcyon Grove, in the early part of the nineteenth century. The exact date of construction is unknown, although Governor Pickens was living in it when he wrote his will in 1817. The unusual use of woodwork is a characteristic of the interior as well as the exterior. The house contains notable examples of handcarved mantels, staircase ornaments and wainscoting. The present owner is Mrs. Percy Marshall Feltham.

PLATE XLIX

GOVERNOR'S MANSION, Columbia. 1855. Since 1868, this white stucco structure has served as a residence for the state's chief executive. It was built as an officers' barracks for the Arsenal Academy, an ante bellum State military school, and was the only building of this institution to survive when Sherman's troops burned Columbia.

PLATE L

THE SOUTH CAROLINIANA LIBRARY, Columbia. 1840. This structure, which dominates the inner campus of the University of South Carolina, was the first separate library building erected by any institution of higher learning in the United States. It now houses an extensive collection of historical material concerning South Carolina. Fireproof wings were added in 1927.

PLATE LI

TRINITY EPISCOPAL CHURCH, Columbia. 1847. The first service of this congregation was held in the original State House in 1812. A frame church was erected in 1814 and the corner stone of the present building was laid in 1846. Edward Brickell White, the architect, based his designs upon a Gothic style church at Yorkminster, England. The transept was added in 1861. The church con-

tains a baptismal font executed by Hiram Powers and imported stained glass windows of exceptional beauty.

PLATE LII

SEIBELS HOUSE, 1601 Richland Street, Columbia. c. 1787. Hand-hewn timbers were used by A. M. Haile to build this Georgian type residence. Carved on a beam in the basement is the date "1787," usually considered the year in which the building was completed. Columns on three sides support a low roof extending over a portico paved with old English tile. Mr. and Mrs. John Jacob Seibels are the present owners.

PLATE LIII

FIRST PRESBYTERIAN CHURCH, Columbia. 1853. The congregation of this church was organized in 1795. It was later housed in a wooden structure brought from Granby across the Congaree River, where it had served as a courthouse of Lexington District. The church yard is the city's oldest burial ground; in it are buried such notables as Jonathan Maxcy, first president of South Carolina College; Ann Pamela Cuningham, saviour of Mount Vernon; and the parents of Woodrow Wilson. The present building is a pure Gothic style structure of unusual distinction.

PLATE LIV

RUINS OF MILLWOOD, near Columbia. Richland County. Prior to 1820. All that remains of this once handsome residence with its extensive formal gardens is four fluted columns. It was built by Col. Wade Hampton, one of the nation's wealthiest planters, in the second decade of the nineteenth century. Colonel Hampton, who bore the message of the defeat of the British at the Battle of New Orleans to President Madison, was the father of the famous Confederate general and governor of the same name. Millwood was burned by Sherman's troops in 1865.

PLATES LVI AND LVII

MULBERRY PLANTATION, near Camden. Kershaw County. 1820. In the days when miasma from the swamps was believed to be the cause of malaria, Colonel James Chesnut built this dwelling as a seasonal residence for his plantation in the Wateree River lowlands. It is approached through an avenue of laurel trees. Mr. and Mrs. David R. Williams are the present owners; he is a descendant of Colonel Chesnut and his famous wife, Mary Boykin Chesnut.

PLATES LVIII AND LIX

BETHESDA PRESBYTERIAN CHURCH, Camden. Kershaw County. 1820. Robert Mills, the architect of this church, described it thus: "A portico of four Doric columns in front and a neat spire in the rear containing the bell . . . the floor and pews rise as they recede from the pulpit, giving every advantage to the audience, both in seeing and hearing." The intricate steps in the rear lead to the slave galleries. The Presbyterians of Camden built their first house of worship about 1771; it was destroyed in the Revolutionary War.